Fun at the Circus

CAROL FALLON

GILL EDUCATION

Contents

Note: 1st Class Readers 1 and 2 cover 18 units of work. For ease of planning, the numbering is consistent with the Skills Book across the two Readers: Reader 1 covers Units 1–9 and Reader 2 covers Units 10–18.

Monkeying Around

My reading goal ★ Talk about the illustrations and the meaning of new words.

When Mam and Dad told Evan about his birthday surprise, he tried hard to be excited.

He liked Dublin Zoo, but he had been there lots of times.

He really wanted to go to the Ireland v South Africa game in the Aviva, but tickets were hard to get.

Evan felt better when he heard Ella's reaction.

"Woohoo!" she shouted.

Mam also said they'd get a banana-split ice cream at the zoo – Evan's favourite!

In the end, Evan's birthday was a day to remember...

The day was sunny.

It was the hottest day of the year.

Evan picked out his hat and shorts that morning with a big smile on his face.

The day before, his friend Leo had told him about the new baby rhino and a **competition** the zoo was running to name her.

Evan had been thinking of lots of names.

He couldn't wait to enter them!

Rex was his top pick so far.

Mam, Dad, Evan and Ella had a fantastic day at the zoo.

They saw elephants taking a bath and two giraffes having a race. They even got to hold a kit! (This is the name for a baby animal – do you know which one?)

Evan couldn't wait to tell Leo all about it.

There were even some hens **fighting** over their food! Peck, peck, peck!

"The early bird gets the worm. Or in this case, the early hen gets the seeds!" joked Dad.

Evan entered the rhino-naming competition.

He had a good feeling about it.

The baby rhino looked like a 'Rex' to him.

The <u>cherry on top of the cake</u> was seeing the monkeys on the monkey bars.

Evan imagined him and his friends swinging just like that, saying, "Ooh ooh, aah aah"!

Time flies when you're having fun and soon it was time to leave the zoo.

Dad took blankets out of the boot. Mam went to get the ice creams.

They all sat down to enjoy a picnic.

Evan's banana-split ice cream was so tasty!

After playing a game of hurling, Mam and Dad said it was time to hit the road.

That was when the fun really began...

Soon, they were home.

Dad parked the car.

"Will you please stop making that noise?" he said to Mam.

It wasn't Mam, so she turned to Evan.

"Stop tapping the seat, Evan," she said.

Evan **shrugged** his shoulders and looked at Ella.

"Stop tapping, Ella!" he said, but Ella was asleep.

Dad, Mam and Evan looked at each other and then BANG!

They looked at the boot.

Everyone jumped out (sleepy Ella too!).

Dad slowly opened the boot.

"What is it?" whispered Ella.

<u>In the blink of an eye</u>, something small and furry jumped out.

It looked at Evan and then ran to the house.

Evan saw a long tail **scurry** in through the cat flap.

Everyone was silent. Then...

"DID A MONKEY RUN INTO MY HOUSE?" shouted Mam. She sat on the grass in shock.

Dad said, "Call the zoo!" and ran after the monkey. Evan ran after Dad.

Dad opened the door. Evan saw the monkey **leaping** around the kitchen, <u>having a whale of a time</u>!

It looked like fun.

Evan wanted to join in!

The monkey got a banana and peeled it.

"Look Dad, he likes bananas too!" said Evan.

Dad and Evan waited outside for the **zookeepers**.

Ella made a fan and waved it in Mam's face.

Evan would have LOVED to take a photo of his mam.

Somehow, he didn't think she would like that!

Besides, he was too busy looking at his visitor.

After the monkey had his banana, he swung from press to press.

It was a cool way to travel!

Before long, two zookeepers from Dublin Zoo came.

They brought the monkey out to the garden.

Bill and Zoe said monkeys were smart, especially **vervet** monkeys from South Africa.

"We'll have to see how Charlie **escaped**," said Zoe.

"Maybe he was trying to go to the South Africa match. He could be their **mascot**," smiled Dad.

Evan had forgotten all about the match. Having a monkey come to visit was far better.

"We're lucky you rang us," said Bill. "Would you like to come to the zoo? You can work with us for the day."

Evan's face lit up.

"Yes please," he said. "This is the best birthday ever!"

Every Time I Climb a Tree
by David McCord

Every time I climb a tree
Every time I climb a tree
Every time I climb a tree
I scrape a leg
Or skin a knee
And every time I climb a tree
I find some ants
Or dodge a bee
And get the ants
All over me.

And every time I climb a tree
Where have you been?
They say to me
But don't they know that I am free
Every time I climb a tree?

Under Henry's Floorboards

My reading goal ★ Clap and count the syllables in the new words.

In March, moving-in day was a busy day.

There were boxes *everywhere*.

Dad fell over one of them and said a word that Mam gave out to him for.

It was funny, but Dad's funny bone didn't think so!

Henry and his family had moved to Dublin.

They lived a long way from his cousin Ella and the Mooney family now.

Dad had a new job.

This meant a new house, a new teacher and new friends for Henry.

Henry's new school would be different to his old one – *very* different.

It made him **nervous**.

His old school was a Gaelscoil.

His teacher there was called Kevin.

Irish was Henry's favourite **subject**.

He spoke in Irish all the time.

He loved doing this with his family.

It was like they had a secret code no one else understood.

"We're secret agents!" his sister always joked.

Henry's new teacher was called Ms Rogers.

The children in his new school didn't speak Irish all the time.

Henry tried not to <u>feel blue</u> about this.

He was sure he would get used to it.

On moving-in day, Henry found something that really made him feel like a secret agent.

Auntie Kate was helping him unpack his bedroom.

"Start with these, Henry," said Auntie Kate, pointing to some boxes. "I'll go outside and get more."

Henry walked to the boxes.

He tripped and fell over, just like Dad.

"Ow!" he said, rubbing his knee.

Henry turned around and saw a **floorboard** sticking up.

He **crawled** over to it and lifted it.

He looked inside.

He rubbed his eyes.

He shook his head.

Under Henry's floorboards... was an EGG!

"Wow!" said Henry.

He looked even closer.

The egg was inside a shoebox.

There was soil all around it.

The soil was warm from the pipes under the floor.

Henry heard Auntie Kate coming back up the stairs.

He gently put the floorboard back down.

He ran to the boxes.

"You don't have much done, Henry," said Auntie Kate. "What have you been doing?"

"Oh, just looking… out the window… at the park. Isn't it **beautiful**?" Henry said, <u>thinking on his feet</u>.

Auntie Kate looked at the park.

Then she looked at Henry.

"Are you sure you feel OK?" she said.

It was raining.

The park was flooded.

"Let's just get started," said Henry.

Henry couldn't wait for Auntie Kate to leave.

As soon as she left, Henry pulled up the floorboard.

"What is this egg doing here?" he **wondered**.

Suddenly, Henry saw a crack.

Then another one, and another... and another!

A head popped out of the egg.

Next, out came a green neck and a hard shell.

Finally, out came four legs.

It was a baby **turtle**.

"Wow!" said Henry.

He looked for his tablet and **typed**: 'how to look after a baby turtle'.

He read that turtles eat fresh **vegetables**. They need to be warm and near water.

Henry ran to the kitchen. He got lettuce and a bowl of water.

He placed the bowl in the soil and left the lettuce there too.

Henry watched his new friend.

He said, "I wonder where you came from?"

He knew he should tell Mam and Dad about the turtle.

But the truth was, Henry was feeling **lonely**.

Now he had a friend to talk to!

"I will name you Squirt," he said.

Henry and Squirt had a lot of fun together.

They had crawling races across the floor.

They ate their vegetables together.

Henry even sang Squirt some songs!

A few days later, Henry began to worry about Squirt.

He wasn't sure if he had enough space or water.

He wondered if he was doing the right thing.

"Is everything OK?" asked Dad one day.

Henry couldn't hold it in.

He showed the baby turtle to Dad.

"Henry, you did the right thing by telling me," said Dad. "But you know what we have to do, don't you?"

Henry knew.

Henry and Dad took Squirt to the see the vet.

The vet was kind.

She told Henry he had taken great care of Squirt.

From now on, Dublin Zoo was going to look after Squirt.

Dad said that Henry could visit him there.

Henry knew turtles should not live under floorboards.

He felt happy that Squirt was going to live with his turtle friends.

Henry and Dad waved goodbye to Squirt.

"What an exciting start to our life in Dublin!" said Dad.

"Who knows what will happen next?" agreed Henry.

The Little Turtle
by Vachel Lindsay

There was a little turtle.

He lived in a box.

He swam in a puddle.

He climbed on the rocks.

He snapped at a mosquito.

He snapped at a flea.

He snapped at a minnow.

And he snapped at me.

He caught the mosquito.

He caught the flea.

He caught the minnow.

But he didn't catch me.

Fun at the Circus

Last week was a super week for Evan and Ella.

Their baby brother, Ed, was born.

Their dad brought them to see Mam and Ed in **hospital**.

Ed was tiny!

The next day, Ella told Tom that Ed was "the world's cutest baby."

She couldn't wait to play dress-up with him.

Evan couldn't wait to play football with him.

On Saturday, the Kelly family went to the circus.

They **invited** Evan and Ella too.

Before they left, Evan and Ella's dad gave them money to buy popcorn.

Tom's parents bought ice cream for everyone too.

Tom, Meg and Mel were so glad to be at the circus with their friends.

They couldn't wait for the show to start.

Tom sat down and looked around.

The circus tent was huge.

There were red and white flags everywhere.

Lights shone on the stage.

All of the seats were full.

"I hope there are clowns," said Tom.

"There always are," said Ella. "I hope they aren't too silly."

"How can clowns be too silly?" asked Tom.

For Tom, you could never be *too* silly, not at the circus!

The music started.

First to arrive were the clowns.

One clown had **rainbow** hair, a rainbow outfit and a rainbow car.

(He called himself the world's most **colourful** man.)

The other clown had the colours of the Irish flag in his hair.

They played tricks on each other.

They pulled balloons from behind their ears.

They squirted water into the crowd.

Tom loved that they were silly.

"They're super silly!" agreed Ella.

The Kelly and Mooney **families** <u>had a ball</u> at the circus.

Evan loved the music.

Meg liked the dancers.

The man on **stilts** was Mel's favourite.

"The jugglers were the best," said Ella.

As for Tom? He thought the clowns were <u>the bee's knees</u>.

He kept thinking about all of their tricks as he left the circus tent.

There was a big crowd walking.

"Tom, pay **attention**!" said Dad.

Tom didn't hear him.

His mind was full of red noses and flowers that squirted water!

Tom's <u>head was in the clouds</u>.

Before long, he was lost.

There were people everywhere.

He couldn't see his parents, sisters or friends.

He didn't know where to go.

He didn't know what to do.

"Mam? Dad?" he called out.

There was no reply.

Tom decided to stay where he was until his parents found him.

That was what Ms Brady had said to do in Stay Safe.

It took a while for the crowd to leave.

Tom was still on his own.

He tried not to worry.

"Are you OK?" a voice asked.

Tom looked behind him and saw 'the world's most colourful man'.

He looked a bit different.

He didn't have his rainbow car.

He wasn't wearing his rainbow jacket.

But he still had all the colours of the rainbow in his hair!

"I'm just waiting for my mam and dad," said Tom.

"I see," said the man. "Would you like to have this while you wait?"

He pulled a rainbow balloon from his ear.

"Yes, please," said Tom.

He held onto it **tightly**.

It looked amazing!

"TOM!"

Tom turned around to see his dad running to him.

"There you are. I was so worried," said Dad.

"Sorry, Dad," said Tom.

Tom's dad saw the balloon.

"Where did you get that?" he asked.

"The world's most colourful man gave it to me. Look..." said Tom, turning to thank him.

The clown had gone.

Tom looked around, but he was nowhere to be seen.

Tom and his dad walked to the **exit**.

Tom held onto his balloon.

He couldn't wait to give it to baby Ed.

After all, the world's cutest baby should have the world's most colourful balloon!

Where Was I?

by Inez Hogan

I saw clowns

Laughing, tumbling.

Bands were playing,

Big drums rumbling.

Seals were tossing

Balls about.

Monkeys swinging

In and out.

Acrobats were

Swinging high,

Elephants parading by.

Can you tell me

Where was I?

Spring Has Sprung

My reading goal ★ Think about why the author wrote this text.

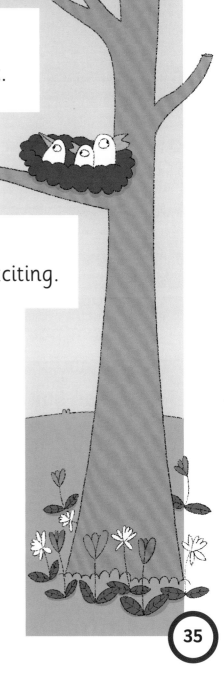

Spring has sprung on Tom and Ella's street.

The birds are singing and the days are longer.

Daffodils are blooming. Leaves are growing on trees.

Everyone is getting ready for something exciting.

Work is about to begin on a new **community** hall.

A market is being held to **raise** money.

All of the money will go towards building the new hall.

Everyone has been asked to make spring crafts to sell at the market.

The Kelly and Mooney families have been hard at work for weeks now.

Ella has been working with her grandad.

They have been making flower **wreaths**.

 # Make a Flower Wreath

What you will need:

A paper plate with the centre cut out
Green paint
A paintbrush
Small bun cases in lots of colours
A pair of **scissors**
Glue
Buttons or gems
Ribbon

Method:

1. Paint the paper plate ring green and leave it to dry.

2. Fold green bun cases in half to make leaves.

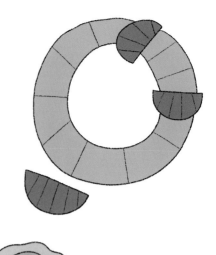

3. Turn the rest of the bun cases inside out. Now the colours are on the inside of the cups.

4. Cut along the tops of the bun cases in a wavy line so that they look more like flowers.

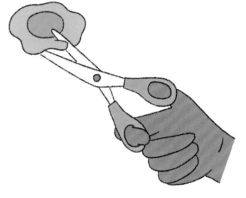

5. Glue the green bun cases onto the paper plate ring. They should stick out over the edge.

6. Glue the rest of the bun cases around the paper plate ring.

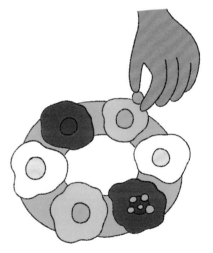

7. Jazz up your flowers by adding a button or a gem in the middle of each.

8. Loop some ribbon onto the back of the paper plate ring.

9. Wait for the wreath to dry fully.

10. Hang it on a door.

Tom and his nana have been making paper trees to welcome spring. They have to make a lot, but Nana is <u>as cool as a **cucumber**</u> about it.

 Make a Paper Tree

What you will need:

Blue, brown, green, dark pink and light pink card
A pair of scissors
A glue stick
A ruler

Method:

1. Cut out a rectangle from the green card. This is the grass.

2. Glue it onto the bottom of the blue card.

3. Cut out a tree trunk and branches from the brown card.

4. Glue them onto the blue card.

5. Cut out small strips of pink and dark pink card. These should be about 2 cm long and you'll need around 40.

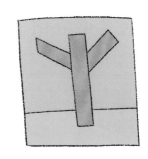

6. Put glue onto one end of a paper strip. Bend it into a ring. Press the two ends together.

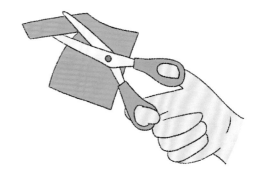

7. Fold and glue all of the paper strips into rings.

8. Put glue onto the bottom of a paper ring and press it onto a branch of the tree.

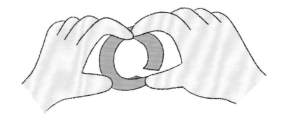

9. Glue all of the paper rings onto the branches of the tree.

10. When the tree is full with paper rings, allow the glue to dry.

11. Hang up the paper tree **craft**.

12. Enjoy all season long.

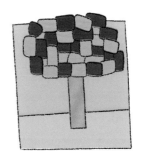

Evan, his dad and his grandad have been working hard on their bird feeders for weeks! Evan says it's <u>as easy as ABC</u>!

 Make a Bird Feeder

What you will need:

Empty plastic milk cartons with lids
A pair of scissors
String
A marker
A ruler
Paints
A paintbrush
Buttons

Method:

1. Use the ruler and marker to draw a medium-sized hole in the middle of the milk carton. (Make sure it's big enough for birds to fit through it.)

2. Cut out the hole using the scissors. Ask an adult for help.

3. Punch a hole at the top of the milk carton.

4. **Thread** string through the hole and tie it with a double **knot**.

5. Paint the milk carton.

6. Use buttons to decorate the outside.

7. Fill the bird feeder with bird seed.

8. Hang it from a tree.

9. Wait for the birds to arrive.

Meg, Mel and Auntie Emma have been making button **bracelets**.

Look how colourful they are!

<u>Fingers crossed</u>, the spring market will be a big success!

 Make Button Bracelets

What you will need:

Buttons
A pair of scissors
String

Method:

1. Choose buttons to make a pattern.

2. Place the string around your wrist to see how much is needed.

3. Use a ruler to add 10 cm more to the length of the string.

4. Tie a knot at the end of the string.

5. Thread a button onto the string.

6. Repeat this until the bracelet is full.

7. Tie the two ends of the string together.

8. Cut off any extra string left over.

Lots of money was raised for the new community hall.

Everyone can't wait for it to open!

My Spring Garden

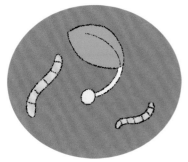

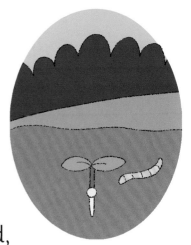

Here is my little garden,

Some seeds I'm going to sow.

Here is my rake to rake the ground,

Here is my handy hoe.

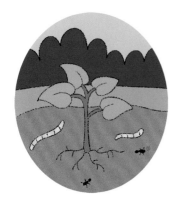

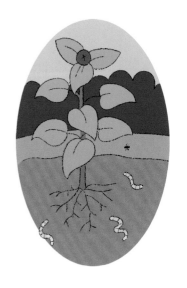

Here is the big, round, yellow sun;

The sun warms everything.

Here are the rain clouds in the sky;

The birds will start to sing.

Little plants will wake up soon,

And lift their sleepy heads;

Little plants will grow and grow

In their little, warm earth beds.

Spring Picnic Planning

14

My reading goal ★ Describe the differences between procedures and other texts.

It's March.

Ms Brady **challenged** First Class to come up with new **recipes** and bring them into school for a spring picnic.

There was only one rule.

The food must be healthy.

No junk food allowed!

First Class want to share them with you.

Here are some of the recipes.

Ella's recipe was **inspired** by one of her favourite books.

 ## Make *The Very Hungry Caterpillar* Sandwiches

Ingredients:	What we need:
12 slices of bread	Toothpicks
Butter	A cutting board
2 slices of ham	A knife
2 slices of chicken	A mini cookie cutter
2 slices of cheese	
1 small tomato	
1 stick of celery	

Method:

1. Put two slices of bread on a cutting board and butter them.

2. Place ham on one slice of bread and then cover it with the other slice.

3. Repeat to make a second ham sandwich, two chicken and two cheese sandwiches.

4. Cut out five circles from each sandwich using a mini cookie cutter.

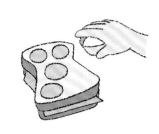

5. Place on a plate in a wiggly shape to make the **caterpillar**'s body.

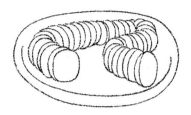

6. Put the tomato at the start of the body. This is the caterpillar's head.

7. Next, cut out two small pieces of cheese for the eyes.

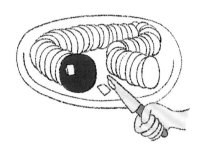

8. Dab them with butter to act as the glue. Then, stick them onto the tomato to start forming the caterpillar's face.

9. Slice small pieces of green celery for the pupils. Use butter to 'glue' them onto the eyes.

10. Cut two long strands from the celery to act as the caterpillar's feelers. Fix them onto the tomato using toothpicks.

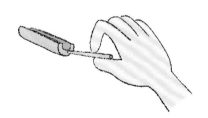

11. Cover your sandwich caterpillar and place it in the fridge.

12. Serve.

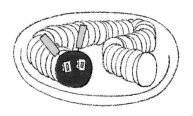

Tom says that these are <u>a piece of cake</u> to make!

 How to Make Apple Turtles

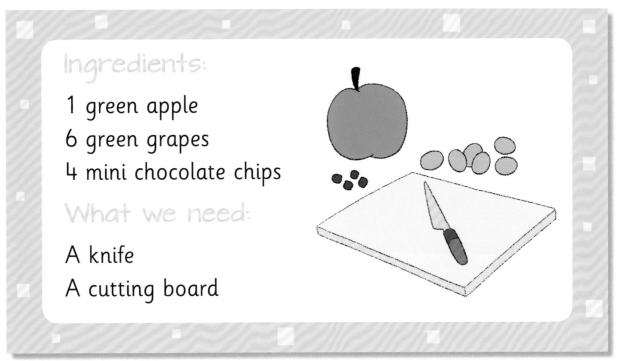

Ingredients:

1 green apple
6 green grapes
4 mini chocolate chips

What we need:

A knife
A cutting board

Method:

1. Wash the apple and the grapes.

2. Slice the apple in half.

3. Cut four grapes in half.

4. Arrange four pieces of grape onto each apple half for the flippers. The fruit will stick together because they are wet.

5. Slice the end off one full grape and use this as the head.

6. **Puncture** two holes in the head using the point of the knife (ask an adult to do this).

7. Turn the chocolate chips pointy side down. Press into the holes for the eyes.

8. Enjoy!

Anna says you'll be <u>as wise as an owl</u> if you eat these!

 Make Rice Cake Owls

Ingredients:

1 slice of meat (chicken or ham)

1 rice cake

1 boiled egg

2 **pumpkin** seeds

1 slice of cheese

2 slices of cucumber

1 carrot stick

What we need:

A knife

A cutting board

Method:

1. Lay the meat on top of the rice cake.

2. Slice the **boiled** egg.

3. Use the two middle slices as eyes.

4. Place pumpkin seeds on the slices of boiled egg. These are the pupils.

5. Cut a small triangle out of the cheese for the beak.

6. Use the cheese to make feet.

7. Cut one cucumber slice in half and use as wings.

8. Arrange on a plate.

9. Make ears using another cucumber slice.

10. Place a carrot stick below the owl. This is a tree branch.

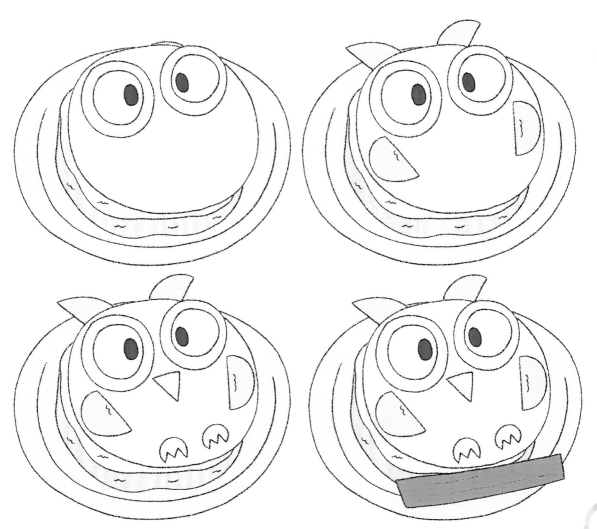

Robbie loves cars, so this was an easy **decision** for him.

 Make Apple Race Car Snacks

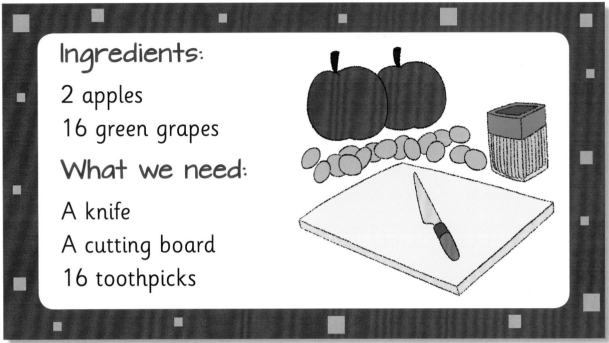

Ingredients:

2 apples
16 green grapes

What we need:

A knife
A cutting board
16 toothpicks

Method:

1. Cut an apple in half.

2. Then, cut the apple half into four pieces. Now you have eight wedges.

3. Stick two toothpicks into each apple wedge to become the car **axles**.

4. Cut the grapes in half.

5. Place the grape halves on each side of the toothpick to make wheels. Vroom vroom!

Top tip: If you aren't going to eat these straight away, then you need to stop the apples from going brown. Drop the cars into a bowl of water with a squeeze of lemon in it. This will help prevent them from **discolouring**.

Ms Brady and First Class hope you liked reading their recipes.

Maybe you'll want to make them yourself.

If so, good luck!

Mom Always Knows

by Bridget Magee

I ask for a cupcake,
Mom says "No."
I take one anyway –
She'll never know.

Under my shirt
The cupcake is hidden.
To my room I sneak,
Where food is forbidden.

I crouch in my closet,
Frilly dresses above.
I quietly indulge
In cupcake love.

Mom's feet appear
Before me as I chew.
I pull a dress over me
To block her view.

Mom says, "I wonder
Where my daughter can be.
And the last cupcake
I was saving for me?"

Competitions Around the World

15

My reading goal ★ As I read, I will track the words with my finger.

Lots of competitions take place every day.

Running, swimming, drawing... I'm sure you have been in some.

But have you heard of the Air **Guitar** World **Championship** in Finland?

What about the Toe Wrestling Championship in England?

Have you come across the Hair Freezing Contest in Canada?

Did you know about the Rock, Paper, Scissors **tournaments** in Japan?

Strange as it may sound, these competitions really do happen!

Let's take a look.

Take Part in the Air Guitar World Championship

The Air Guitar World Championship takes place in Finland.

People pretend they are playing a guitar.

The competition is about having fun.

What you need:

Music
25 euro

Method:

1. Pick a song.

2. Plan your moves to go with the song.

3. Pay the fee to enter (25 euro).

4. Travel to Finland.

5. Perform air guitar to your song.

6. Perform air guitar to an **unknown** song.

7. Wait and see who wins!

The winner takes home a new guitar.

How to Take Part in the Toe Wrestling Championship

The Toe Wrestling Championship takes place in England every summer.

It is like arm **wrestling**, except with feet.

This championship really keeps you on your toes!

What you need:
Toes and feet

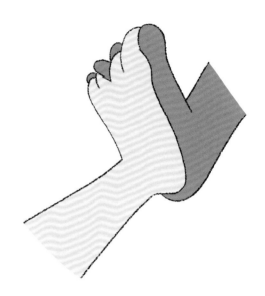

Method:

1. Players take off their socks and shoes.

2. A doctor checks their feet.

3. A player's foot must lie flat against the other person's.

4. Players link toes and must try to trap the other's foot.

5. They start on the right foot.

6. Then, they play with the left foot.

7. Finally, they play with the right foot again if a tie-break is needed.

The best toe wrestler takes home a **trophy**.

Take Part in the Hair Freezing Contest

The Hair Freezing Contest takes place in Canada.

It happens every winter in a place where there are hot springs.

A hot spring is hot water that comes from the earth.

People come to Canada from around the world to take part.

What you need:

A swimsuit

A towel

A camera

Method:

1. Go to the hot springs when the weather is cold. (The **temperature** can drop as low as minus 20!)

2. Change into a swimsuit.

3. Get into the water.

4. Dip your head into the water.

5. Lift your head out of the water.

6. Allow the cold air to slowly freeze your hair. All hair will freeze – eyebrows and eyelashes too!

7. Wait.

8. When your hair begins to freeze, **style** it into shape.

9. Wait some more.

10. Let your hair completely freeze. It will become white.

11. Take a photo.

12. **Dunk** your hair into the hot spring again. It will turn back to normal.

13. Give the photo to the judges.

The person with the best frozen hairstyle wins money.

Take Part in a Rock, Paper, Scissors Tournament

Japan hosts Rock, Paper, Scissors tournaments.

This is a very **popular** game in Japan.

You can try this one in the playground!

What you need:

Hands

Money

Method:

1. Fill in the entry form.

2. Pay the fee.

3. Face the other player.

4. Say, "Rock, paper, scissors."

5. Reveal your hand.

6. Players play **knockout** rounds until there is a winner.

7. The prize is a trophy.

Rock crushes scissors.

Scissors cuts paper.

Paper covers rock.

Psst, here is a tip to help you win!
Wear fancy dress to distract the other players.
One year the winner dressed up as a goose!

Would you like to enter any of these competitions?

Aim High to the Sky
by James McDonald

Aim high to the sky,
In all that you do.
Because you just never know,
What it takes to be you.
Be strong and be brave,
But at the same time be kind.
And always be sure,
That you're using your mind.

Letters Between Friends

16

My reading goal ★ Add expression to my voice as I read.

First Class have been learning about life in Brazil.

Brazil is a country in South **America**.

It is the fifth largest country in the world.

In October, Ms Brady paired up with a school there.

Everyone in First Class has a pen pal from Brazil.

They have been writing to their pen pals all year.

Ella's pen pal is a girl called Maria.

Robbie is writing to a boy named Pedro.

They have been having a lot of fun getting to know somebody from a different country.

Rio de Janeiro, Brazil

Take a look at some of their letters!

Cork,
Ireland
November 3rd

Dear Maria,

How are you? It's good to talk to you! We are back in school after the midterm holidays. Three days ago, it was Hallowe'en. I dressed up as a cat. Mam drew **whiskers** on my face and put cat ears on my head. I got a lot of sweets trick-or-treating this year. Mam said my teeth would rot if I ate them all, so I shared them with Evan. Do you celebrate Hallowe'en in Brazil?

Trick-or-treating

We have been busy in school. We went on a trip to a fire station. It was a lot of fun. We saw all of the fire engines, talked to the firefighters and played with the hoses. Tom **accidentally** sprayed Ms Brady with the hose and she got a bit wet. He felt bad, but Ms Brady said she needed a shower anyway! It was very funny. Ms Brady is a kind teacher.

The bell is about to go for lunch, so I have to finish my letter.

Talk to you soon!

From,

Ella

A fire station in Ireland

Rio de Janeiro,
Brazil
December 23rd

Hi Ella,

I am great. I hope you are good too. I liked reading your letter. Poor Ms Brady! I hope she didn't get *too* wet. It is summer in Brazil. Last week, it was very hot. I would have liked a water hose to cool me down! We went on a trip too. We went to a soccer camp. Soccer is a popular sport in Brazil. We have won the World Cup five times. I love to play soccer. The camp was a lot of fun. I scored a goal and my team won. Woohoo!

With my friend from soccer camp!

The carnival parade
in Rio de Janeiro

We have Hallowe'en in Brazil, but it is not a big holiday. I dressed up as a pumpkin and one lady gave me pumpkin seeds. They won't rot my teeth, but I would have liked sweets more! **Carnival** is the biggest celebration here. It happens before Lent. Carnival is one big party. This year it was so much fun. School was closed and everyone dressed up and danced in the streets. There were colourful **parades** and loud music. Take a look at the photo my mam printed for me. Maybe one day you will come to Brazil and see Carnival in real life!

Bye for now,

Maria

Rio de Janeiro,
Brazil
March 25th

Hi Robbie,

Olá from Brazil! Sorry my letter is late. It was my birthday last week and I had a lot to do. I had a cake. It was in the shape of a football. In Brazil, the birthday boy or girl gives the first slice of cake to a special person. I gave the first slice to my mam. We had pizza, hot dogs and popcorn at the party. My favourite present was a **bicycle**. It's green, blue and yellow, just like our flag. It's a super fast bike!

My birthday cake

A pink river dolphin

I went on a trip to the zoo with my friends. Have you heard of the Amazon **Rainforest**? It is the biggest rainforest in the world and part of it is in Brazil. We have lots of cool animals in Brazil. We saw some of them at the zoo. There were eels, snakes, **poison** dart frogs and sloths. There was also a butterfly house. My favourite animal was the pink river **dolphin**. It really is pink! My sister wants one as a pet. My dad said maybe, but I think he might have been <u>spinning a yarn</u>. I had a fantastic day. It was my best birthday ever!

I am happy we share a birthday. I can't wait to hear all about yours!

Bye for now,

Pedro

Cork,
Ireland
April 10th

Hi Pedro,

Happy birthday! Sounds like your birthday was a lot of fun. I like that we share the same birthday :) I also love that it's the same day as Saint Patrick's Day! I had the day off school for my birthday. I always get the day off, because Saint Patrick's Day is a **national** holiday here. I went to a parade and then a hurling match in Croke Park. I had a cake too. It was in the colours of the Irish flag – green, white and orange. I think my cake and your bike would look great together!

Saint Patrick's Day parade in Dublin

Inside Croke Park Stadium

I bet my dog Star would love to see the pink dolphin at the zoo. She has a dolphin teddy that she chews all the time. She goes <u>bug-eyed</u> every time she sees it! We bought it for Ella's brother Ed, but Star won't let it go. I would love to go to Brazil some day. Dad says maybe we'll go when I'm older. I hope he isn't lying! This year we're going to Spain on our holidays. I can't wait to swim in the sea and play in the sand.

I will take photos and send you one.

Talk to you soon.

Your friend,

Robbie

Foreign Lands
by Robert Louis Stevenson

Up into the cherry tree
Who should climb but little me?
I held the trunk with both my hands
And looked abroad in foreign lands.

I saw the next door garden lie,
Adorned with flowers, before my eye,
And many pleasant places more
That I had never seen before.

Ella the Writer

17

My reading goal ★ Point out the different parts of a book: the title, the spine, the author, the illustrator and the blurb.

It is almost time for Ella to go on her holidays.

The Mooneys are going to Kerry.

It will be their first holiday as a family of five.

Baby Ed is four months old now.

He smiles a lot.

Ella thinks he is the **happiest** baby in the world, except at night-time.

Ed doesn't always sleep when he should.

Since baby Ed arrived, Mam and Dad have been really busy.

A few days before they left for their holiday, Mam asked Ella to help her.

She wrote a list for Ella and asked her to check that she had everything ready.

Ella loved lists.

She felt super important reading all of the things she had to do.

Ella's To-do List

1. Finish packing.
2. Email Nana Mooney.
3. Write Tom's birthday card.
4. Help Dad make a beach game.

First things first: Ella had to finish packing. Mam helped her write a **checklist**.

They tried to remember all the things Ella would need on her holidays.

Here's what Mam and Ella came up with:

Ella's Holiday Checklist

T-shirts ☐   shorts ☐   underwear ☐

vests ☐   socks ☐   **swimsuit** ☐

jeans ☐   dresses ☐   shoes ☐

books ☐   toys ☐   sunglasses ☐

Ella spent the afternoon finding all the things she needed.

Auntie Liz called over and helped her.

It didn't take long before they were finished.

"All done," said Ella, zipping up her suitcase.

"Super!" replied Mam. "What's next on your list?"

"Number two is writing an email to Nana Mooney," said Ella.

Nana Mooney had gone to visit some of her friends in London.

She had asked Ella to email her before she left on her holidays.

Ella sat down with her tablet and began to type...

To: nanamooney@gmail.com

Subject: Holiday time

Dear Nana,

How are you? It is 2 o'clock and I have finished packing my suitcase for my holidays. I am so excited! Mam says there are two sleeps left until we go. I hope you are having a nice time in London with your friends. What is the best thing about London? Is the weather nice? It is raining here today, but Dad says the sun is going to shine on our trip. I really hope it does. Evan always <u>stirs up a **hornet's** nest</u> when he's indoors for too long.

The beach isn't much fun in the rain! I want to build sandcastles, go swimming in the sea and find a shell to give to baby Ed. Fingers crossed!

Mam gave me a to-do list and writing this email was the second thing on it. My next job is to write Tom's birthday card. I'll miss his birthday party, but Mam said he can come over for a **sleepover** soon.

See you when I'm home!

Love,

Ella

Mam read over Ella's email and pressed 'send'.

"Tom's birthday card is next," said Ella.

Ella found Tom's card in the drawer. It had a picture of an astronaut inside.

It was the perfect card for Tom, because that's what he wanted to be when he was older.

Ella got her pencil and wrote the card...

To Tom,
Happy birthday!
I hope you have a great day.
Don't miss me *too* much at your party!
See you when I get back from Kerry.
From,
Ella

Ella put the card into the **envelope**.

Dad helped her wrap Tom's birthday present.

It was a spacesuit for Luna the dog.

It matched the one Tom already had for himself.

Dad and Ella put the card and the present in a safe place.

"You can give them to Tom before we leave," said Dad.

"Now I can help you with the beach game!" replied Ella.

The Mooneys all loved the beach, but Ella enjoyed it the most.

She liked the sound of the waves and the sand between her toes.

She was always on the lookout for shells. She had a big **collection** already.

She hoped to find a large shell. One that let you hear the sound of the ocean when you held it to your ear.

Ella and Dad thought about all the things they might find on the beach.

They decided to make a beach **scavenger** hunt.

This is what they came up with:

Beach Scavenger Hunt

beach ball ☐   sandcastle ☐   deck chair ☐

umbrella ☐   seashell ☐   wave ☐

seaweed ☐   pebble ☐   **suncream** ☐

goggles ☐   flip-flops ☐   surfboard ☐

"This looks wonderful, Ella," said Dad.

Ella ticked off job number four on her list.

"Bob's your uncle!" she said. "I'm ready for my holidays."

Ella showed the list to Mam.

"Wow, you really are ready, Ella," said Mam. "We are going to have a fantastic time in Kerry!"

Sandy Beaches
by Morgan Swain

Sprinkle, squish between my toes,

The smell of ocean to my nose.

I can feel each grain of sand,

It falls from air into my hand.

The shells I find along the shore,

Picked up by birds that fly and soar.

They sparkle like the ocean's waves,

And carry sand from all the lakes.

I walk along the tip of the sea,

That's where my feet leave prints to be.

I walk all the way to the end of the land,

The land that holds this beautiful sand.

First Class Postcards

18

My reading goal ★ Choose a favourite genre and share my reasons.

It is June and the summer holidays are on the way.

Ms Brady has to pack up her classroom.

She will be teaching Third Class next year.

Her classroom is colourful.

There are books everywhere!

There is art on the walls.

There are lots of **postcards** on the wall behind Ms Brady's desk.

These are from children who went on trips during the year.

The children were lucky this year.

They went on nice holidays.

Every time they went away, they sent a postcard to their class.

It was kind of like the Flat Stanley Project.

For First Class, it became a **tradition**.

Ms Brady takes down a different postcard every day and reads it to the class.

It is fun to remember all of the wonderful things that happened this year.

Let's read some of them.

September 3rd

Hi everyone!

I hope your first day back at school was a good one. Did Ms Brady give you homework? I'm on my holidays in Spain. I'm writing this on the beach. We swim in the sea a lot. It's really hot here. Dad gives us ice cream to cool down. I've had *sooooo* much already. The strawberry one is my favourite. I have to put suncream on every day. I 'helped' Mam put suncream on her back yesterday. I used the suncream to draw a smiley face on her skin, but I didn't cover the rest of her back. Her skin got **burned**. Now she has a white smiley face on a red back! Dad said he liked it, but I think that was **tongue** in cheek. Mam says we will be back in Ireland in two more sleeps. See you then!

From Lainey

Happy Hallowe'en!   October 31st

I am in Galway for the midterm break. I am having a spooky time. We are going trick-or-treating later. I wanted to dress up as a witch again. I love my dress! I wanted Evan to dress up as my cat. Last night, I tried to paint whiskers on his face, but he woke up after I drew the first one. He wasn't happy, especially when he tried to wash it off. I had used a **permanent** marker by mistake. It took a LONG time for it to come off. Evan is cross with me. Dad thinks I should have asked him first. Evan said he'll dress up as my cat <u>when pigs fly</u>. Oh well, maybe I will dress up as a cat instead of a witch.

See you all next week.

From Ella

December 22nd

Dear Ms Brady and First Class,

Happy Christmas! We made it to New York. The flight was long. We were on the **aeroplane** for eight hours. I sat beside my nana and we read **comics** together. There were funny movies and yummy snacks too. I was glad when we landed in America. It was snowing. Dad and I had a snowball fight before we got into a taxi. There was so much snow. We've been to Times Square and visited **Central** Park. There are Christmas lights everywhere. I got to see my new baby cousin yesterday. His name is Andy. I held him and gave him a hug. Mam took a photo of us. I brought him a teddy bear from Ireland. I'm going to visit him again today.

See you when I'm back.

From Robbie

To Ms Brady and First Class,   April 24th

We are spending Easter in Dublin. We are having a great time. We are here for two days. It rained yesterday, so we went to the pool. Afterwards, it was still raining, so Dad brought us to the cinema. We had popcorn. It **reminded** me of our classroom cinema when we were snowed in at school! The seats were very comfortable in the cinema. I had a full row to myself! Dad, Meg and Mel sat behind me. I don't know what we are doing today. Mam is having a nap, Dad is reading the newspaper and the twins are watching television. We call this 'chill-out time'. Oh wait, Dad just said we're going to the zoo. I'll look out for Charlie, Ella!

See you next week.

From Tom

June 22nd

To First Class,

Hello, everyone. **Greetings** from London! I am having a lovely time. The sun is shining here. I'm using lots of suncream, Lainey! I went to see a show and I visited the palace too. I even saw Big Ben. I am going shopping today. I am looking for new sunglasses. My pineapple ones broke – I sat on them on the plane. Which sunglasses do you think I should buy next? Strawberry ones? Cat ones? Maybe I'll get heart-shaped ones! Soon it will be the last week of school. I hope you all have a wonderful summer. Call into my classroom next year to say hello!

See you soon.

From Ms Brady

Summer Morning
by Rachel Field

I saw dawn creep across the sky,

And all the gulls go flying by.

I saw the sea put on its dress

Of blue midsummer loveliness,

And heard the trees begin to stir

Green arms of pine and juniper.

I heard the wind call out and say:

"Get up, my dear, it is today!"